The UK NINJA Dual Zone

Air Fryer Recipe Book

Simple, Delicious, Family Friendly British Recipes Using Easy To Find Ingredients

Mildred Charlton

BALVAIRD
PUBLISHING

BALVAIRD PUBLISHING

Balvaird Publishing LLC
30 N Gould St Ste 32278
Sheridan, WY 82801

Author: Mildred Charlton
Editor: Hanley Knight
Illustrator: Glen Franklin

ISBN 978-1-960797-07-0 (Paperback).
ISBN 978-1-960797-06-3 (eBook).

INTRODUCTION

I'm Mildred a Brit. I'm so excited to share some of my favorite Ninja Foodi dual zone recipes with you. Whether you're an experienced or a beginner user, I'm sure you'll find something you love. I've included a variety of recipes, from classic British mains to delicious desserts. With clear instructions, helpful tips, British English terminologies and inspiring photos, and only including ingredients that are available to buy from UK supermarkets, you'll be able to create delicious meals in no time. So, let's get cooking!

Mildred Charlton

NINJA FOODI DUAL ZONE 101

MAKE MANY DELICIOUS MEALS WITH EASE.

The Ninja Foodi Dual Zone air fryer is an amazing kitchen appliance that can help you make many delicious meals with ease. It can air fry, bake, roast, max crisp and dehydrate. With the Ninja Dual air fryer 2 cooking zones, you can cook different foods at the same time. It's perfect for busy households that don't have a lot of time to prepare meals.

EXPERT GUIDANCE ON HOW TO USE YOUR NINJA DUAL ZONE

In this guide I'll guide you through everything you need to know, including how it works, the best foods to air fry, how to clean it, and other useful hints for making the most of your Ninja Dual Zone air fryer! and will leave you feeling confident to get you started in the kitchen .

>>>>>

4

USING YOUR Dual Zone FUNCTIONS

1. The Dual Zone Technology:

You can cook the same food in each zone with the same function, use **MATCH** to automatically duplicate settings In Zone 1 and Zone 2.

You can cook two separate dishes in two different ways (choose from six functions) at the same time, then **SYNC** them to finish at the exact appropriate time so that everything arrives at the table hot.

The Ninja Foodi Dual Zone mode includes 6 functions:

- *MAX CRISP* : Ideal for frozen foods such as Chips and Fish fingers.

- *AIR FRY* : Cooks food quickly without drying it out. For guilt-free fried foods that are moist and juicy on the inside while remaining crispy on the outside.

- *ROAST* : Use your Ninja Foodi Dual Zone air fryer as Conventional oven to roast meats.

- *REHEAT* : Warming leftovers gently will bring them back to life, resulting in crispy results.

- *DEHYDRATE* : Dehydrate fruits and vegetables for delicious snacks or dehydrate herbs to reduce food waste.

- *BAKE* : Make fluffy cakes, scones, biscuits and breads at home.

Getting Started

Here are some basic Tips When Using The Ninja Dual Zone Air Frye:

1. *Always place your Ninja Dual Zone Air Fryer* on a flat, heat-resistant surface, and leave at least 13-cm of space behind the air fryer for the exhaust vent.

2. *Don't overcrowd the drawers.* Over-crowding the drawers will prevent foods from crisping and browning evenly and take longer cooking time .

3. *Occasionally shake the ingredients while air frying.* Open the drawers and shake or toss the ingredients for even browning. When finished, reinsert drawers and continue cooking.

4. *Check the doneness of your food as many times as you want.* This is one of the nicest features of the Ninja dual zone air fryers: you can open the drawer at any time during the cooking time to check on the cooking process. The cooking process will resume where it left off when you reinsert the drawers into the air fryer.

5. *Clean the drawer* as well as the crisping plates after every use.

6. *Reduce the temperature by 10°C* when converting recipes from a conventional oven to Ninja Dual Zone Air Fryer . To avoid overcooking, check the food frequently .

⚠️ NOTICE

Always refer to your specific Ninja Dual Zone Air Fryer model's manual for detailed instructions and safety precautions.

Cleaning the Ninja Dual Zone Drawers and Crisping Plates:

- Clean the Drawers and the Crisping plates after every use. But let The Unit Cool Down first before you start to clean it.

- The Drawers and the Crisping plates are dishwasher-safe, but hand washing is recommended because it protects the Non-Stick coating.

- If there is a lot of oil and residue on the crisper plate, or drawers, soak them in warm, soapy water.

- If scrubbing is required, use a non-abrasive sponge to avoid scratching or damaging the nonstick coating.

- To clean the outside of your Ninja Dual Zone, Wipe with damp cloth. NEVER immerse the main unit in water or any other liquid.

Best Ninja Dual Zone Air Fryer Accessories:

Tips When Choosing Ninja Dual Zone Air Fryer Accessories:

- *Any bakeware marked "oven safe" will work with Ninja Dual Zone air fryers.*

- *Choose Bakeware or baking dishes with No Handles*

- *Know your Ninja Dual Zone air fryer drawer's INTERIOR size, not its total capacity.*

My Favorite Baking Dishes for Ninja Dual Zone Air Fryer:

1 lb Loaf Tin

Silicone Tongs

Silicone Muffin Cups

Small Tart Tins

CONTENTS

Breakfast

Delicious everyday breakfasts and amazing brunches.

Carmalised Onion and Cheese Quiche

Carmalised Onion and Cheese Quiche

Serves : 6   Prep Time : 20 Mins   Cook Time : 15 Mins

Ingredients

For the crust:

- 200g plain flour
- ½ tsp salt
- 100g cold butter, cut into cubes
- 1 large egg
- Cold water, as needed

Filling:

- 1 large onion, thinly sliced
- 4 tbsp water
- 150g grated cheddar cheese
- 4 large eggs
- 100ml milk
- 200ml double cream
- Salt and pepper to taste

Recipe tip:

Pie crust: For a head start use a store-bought pie crust.

Method

1. In a bowl, add flour, butter, salt and rub with hands into the flour until resembles breadcrumbs. Add the egg and 1 tbsp water at a time, mix then bring together in a ball (if its too dry add more water, 1 tbsp at a time).

2. On a floured surface roll the dough into 1/2-cm thickness. Grease 6 individual pie dishes and line with pie crust. Refrigerate.

3. With no crisping plate installed, place onion, water and pinch of salt in the Zone 1 drawer and stir to combine.

4. Select Zone 1, select BAKE, set temperature to 160°C, and set time to 15 minutes. Press the START/PAUSE button to begin cooking.(When time reaches 10 minutes, remove drawer from unit and stir. Reinsert drawer to continue cooking).

5. When cooking is complete, transfer onions to a bowl. Then add eggs, milk, cream, cheddar , salt, and pepper.

6. Pour the egg mixture into refrigerated pie crusts. Place pie dishes in zone 1 & 2 drawers (with crisper plate inserted), then insert drawers in unit.

7. Select Zone 1, select BAKE, set temperature to 160°C and set time to 15 minutes. Select MATCH. Press START/STOP to begin.
When the cooking is complete, let set for 5 minutes, then serve.

Carmalised Onion and Cheese Quiche

For your next special breakfast, brunch, lunch, or supper, make this rich, delicious caramelised onion quiche. Made with flavorful Cheddar cheese, it's sure to be a new favourite.

Sausage and Hash Brown Breakfast Casserole

Serves : 2   Prep Time : 5 Mins   Cook Time : 25 Mins

Ingredients

- 200g grated potatoes
- 150g frozen broccoli florets
- 2 sausages, cut into bite sized pieces
- 4 large eggs
- 2 tbsp milk
- 4 tbsp grated cheddar cheese
- 1 red bell pepper, finely chopped
- Salt and pepper to taste

Method

1. Brush zone 1 and 2 drawers (without a crisping plate inserted) with oil, and line base with a piece of baking parchment.

2. Divide grated potatoes and sausage pieces evenly among the two drawers, sprinkle with oil. Insert drawers in unit. Select Zone 1, select AIR FRY, set temperature to 195°C and set time to 12 minutes. Select MATCH. Press START/STOP to begin. (When time reaches 6 minutes, remove drawers from unit and shake drawers. Reinsert drawers to continue cooking).

3. In a bowl add eggs, milk, cheese, bell pepper, broccoli, salt, and pepper, mix until combined.

4. When the cooking is complete, pour egg mixture over the hash brown in Zone 1 and 2 drawers. Insert both drawers into unit.

5. Select Zone 1, select BAKE, set temperature to 160°C and set time to 13 minutes. Select MATCH. Press START/STOP to begin. When the cooking is complete, let set for 5 minutes, then serve.

12

Baked Sweet Potatoes

Serves : 2   Prep Time : 5 Mins   Cook Time : 40 Mins

Ingredients

- 2 medium sized sweet potatoes

Method

1. Pierce the sweet potatoes all over with a fork. Insert a crisper plate in Zone 1 drawer. Place the sweet potatoes in the drawer.

2. Select Zone 1, select AIR FRY, set temperature to 190°C, and set time to 35-40 minutes. Press the START/PAUSE button to begin cooking. When the cooking is complete, split the sweet potatoes in half open and serve with your favourite toppings.

Jacket Potatoes

Serves : 2   Prep Time : 5 Mins   Cook Time : 40 Mins

Ingredients

- 2 (350g each) King Edward or Maris Piper potato
- 1 tbsp oil
- Salt and pepper to taste

Method

1. Pierce the potatoes all over with a fork. Rub the potatoes with oil. Season with salt and pepper. Insert a crisper plate in Zone 1 drawer. Place the potatoes in the drawer.

2. Select Zone 1, select AIR FRY, set temperature to 200°C, and set time to 40 minutes. Press the START/PAUSE button to begin cooking. When the cooking is complete, slice open each potato, and serve with desired toppings.

Kedgeree

Serves : 4   **Prep Time : 10 Mins**   **Cook Time : 30 Mins**

Ingredients

- 200g uncooked long grain rice
- 20g unsalted butter
- 1 onion, finely chopped
- 1 tbsp curry powder
- 250g smoked haddock, poached in boiling water for 5 mins
- 400ml chicken stock
- 4 large eggs
- Salt & pepper to taste

Method

1. With no crisping plate installed, place rice, stock, butter, onion, curry powder, salt and pepper in the Zone 1 drawer and stir to combine. Insert drawer in unit

2. Insert the crisper plates in Zone 2 drawer. Place eggs on crisper plate. Insert drawer in unit.

3. Select Zone 1, select BAKE, set temperature to 200°C and set time for 30 minutes. Select Zone 2, select AIR FRY, set temperature to 150°C, and set time to 15 minutes. Select SYNC. Press the START/PAUSE button to begin cooking.

4. When cooking is complete, remove eggs and place in a bowl of iced water for a minute, Peel the eggs and cut in quarters. Flake the fish, then add it to rice and stir until gently heated through. Serve with eggs.

Chickpea Baked Eggs

Serves : 4   Prep Time : 10 Mins   Cook Time : 25 Mins

Method

Ingredients

- 1 onion, finely chopped
- 3 tbsp water
- 1 red bell pepper, chopped
- 2 garlic cloves, minced
- 1 tsp smoked paprika
- 1 (400g) tin chopped tomatoes
- 400g tin chickpeas, rinsed and drained
- 4 large eggs
- Salt & pepper to taste

1. With no crisping plate installed, place all ingredients (except eggs) in the Zone 1 drawer and stir to combine.

2. Select Zone 1, select BAKE, set temperature to 200°C, and set time to 15 minutes. Press the START/PAUSE button to begin cooking.(When time reaches 10 minutes, remove drawer from unit and stir. Reinsert drawer to continue cooking).

3. When cooking is complete, remove drawers and make 4 wells in tomato mixture. Crack one egg in each well. Season with salt and pepper. Reinsert drawers.

4. Select Zone 1, select BAKE, set temperature to 170°C and set time for 7 minutes. Press the START/PAUSE button to begin cooking.
When cooking is complete, remove drawers and serve with crusty bread.

Sausage and Egg Casserole

Serves : 4   Prep Time : 5 Mins   Cook Time : 23 Mins

Ingredients

- 1 medium onion, finely chopped
- 3 sausages, cut into bite size pieces
- 3 tbsp crumbled Stilton
- 6 eggs
- 4 tbsp double cream
- ½ tsp garlic powder
- Salt and pepper to taste

Method

1. With no crisping plate installed, place sausage, and onion in the Zone 1 and 2 drawers and stir to combine.

2. Select Zone 1, select AIR FRY, set temperature to 200°C, and set time to 10 minutes. Select MATCH. Press the START/PAUSE button to begin cooking.(When time reaches 5 minutes, remove drawers from unit and stir. Reinsert drawers to continue cooking).

3. In a bowl, add eggs, double cream, garlic powder, stilton, salt and pepper. Mix until combined.

4. When the cooking is complete, pour egg mixture over the sausage and vegetables in Zone 1 and 2 drawers. Insert both drawers into unit.

5. Select Zone 1, select BAKE, set temperature to 160°C and set time to 13 minutes. Select MATCH. Press START/STOP to begin.
When the cooking is complete, let set for 5 minutes, then serve.

Corned Beef Hash Breakfast

🍽 **Serves : 2**   🥣 **Prep Time : 10 Mins**   🍲 **Cook Time : 20 Mins**

Ingredients

- 500g potatoes, peeled and cut into ½-cm cubes
- 1 onion, finely chopped
- 1 garlic clove, minced
- 340g tin corned beef, finely chopped
- 1 tbsp oil
- 2 eggs
- Salt and pepper to taste

Method

1. Toss the potatoes and onion in oil and divide potatoes and onion mixture between in zone 1 & 2 drawers (with crisper plate inserted), then insert drawers in unit.

2. Select zone 1 and zone 2, select AIR FRY and set temp to 200°C and set time to 15 min. Press the START/ STOP button to begin cooking. When zone 1 time reaches 8 minutes, remove drawers from unit and shake drawer for 10 seconds. Reinsert drawer to continue cooking.

3. Remove drawers. Add the corned beef, stir. Select AIR FRY and set temp to 200°C and set time to 5 min. Press the START/ STOP button to begin cooking.

4. Remove drawers. Make a well in each corned beef hash mixture. Crack an egg into each one. Sprinkle with salt and pepper.

5. Place drawers back into unit. Set temp to 185°C and set time to 3 min. Press the START/ STOP button to begin cooking.

6. Scoop out one egg and the corned beef hash into a plate. Repeat with remaining egg and hash for second serving.

Corned Beef Fritters

🍽 Serves : 4   🥣 Prep Time : 5 Mins   🍲 Cook Time : 8 Mins

Ingredients

- 2 eggs
- 340g tinned corned beef, cut into 1-cm cubes
- 100g self raising flour
- 50g breadcrumbs
- 1 tbsp onion powder
- 3 tbsp oil
- Salt and pepper to taste

Method

1. In a large bowl, add the flour, breadcrumbs, onion powder, salt, pepper and mix. Add in eggs and whisk until all combined. Add the corned beef . Stir gently .

2. Use the scoop to add portions of the batter into a sheet pan and flatten slightly to get an even thickness (make 12 fritters). Place in freezer for 20 minutes.

3. Add the fritters in a single layer in zone 1 & 2 drawers (with crisper plate inserted), then insert drawers in unit. Select zone 1 and zone 2, select Air Fry, set temperature to 200°C and set time to 10 minutes until golden, flipping halfway through

4. Sprinkle the fritters with salt if desired and serve.

Baked Porridge Cups

🔔 Serves : 12 cup   Prep Time : 5 Mins   Cook Time : 25 Mins

Ingredients

- 350ml milk
- 2 eggs
- 120ml golden syrup
- 60g melted unsalted butter
- 2 bananas, mashed or 120g yogurt
- 50g dried fruits or mixed nuts
- 250g porridge oats
- 1 tsp baking powder
- 1 tsp ground cinnamon
- Pinch of salt

Method

1. Grease 12 individual silicone muffin cups.

2. In a bowl, add all ingredients and mix until combined. Spoon porridge mixture evenly into muffin cups. Fill all the way to the top.

3. Insert the crisper plates in zone 1 and 2 drawers. Place muffin cups on crisper plate. Insert drawers in unit.

4. Select Zone 1, select AIR FRY, set temperature to 175°C and set time to 25 minutes. Select MATCH. Press START/STOP to begin.

5. When cooking is complete, remove from unit and cool for 10 minutes before serving.

Cheese on Toast

Serves : 2-4   Prep Time : 2 Mins   Cook Time : 8 Mins

Ingredients

- 4 white bread slices
- Softened butter
- 150 g grated cheddar cheese
- Worcestershire sauce

Method

1. Butter one side of bread slices with softened butter.

2. Insert the crisper plates in zone 1 and 2 drawers. Place bread slices on crisper plates. Select Zone 1, select AIR FRY, set temperature to 175°C and set time to 2 minutes. Select MATCH. Press START/STOP to begin.

3. When cooking is complete, remove drawers from unit and add cheese on top of each bread slice, press down the cheese onto the bread and add a few drops of Worcestershire sauce on top. Reinsert drawers to unit.

4. Select Zone 1, select AIR FRY, set temperature to 175°C and set time to 6 minutes. Select MATCH. Press START/STOP to begin.
When cooking is complete, serve immediately.

Broccoli and Mushroom Omelette

Serves : 4   Prep Time : 3 Mins   Cook Time : 7 Mins

Ingredients

- 4 large eggs
- 1 small tomato, chopped
- 50g frozen broccoli florets, thawed
- 50g button mushroom, sliced
- 40g of your favourite grated cheese
- 6 tbsp milk
- Salt and pepper to taste

Method

1. In a bowl, add all ingredients and whisk until combined.

2. With no crisping plate installed, grease Zone 1 and 2 drawers. Then pour egg mixture into both drawers evenly.

3. Select Zone 1, select BAKE, set temperature to 160°C, and set time to 7 minutes. Select MATCH. Press the START/PAUSE button to begin cooking.

4. When cooking is complete, serve.

Celeriac Rosti

🔔 Serves : 4   🥣 Prep Time : 10 Mins   🍲 Cook Time : 13 Mins

Ingredients

- 600g celeriac, peeled and grated
- 2 large eggs
- 1 small onion, finely chopped
- 5 tbsp plain flour
- Salt and pepper to taste

Method

1. In a large bowl, add all ingredients and mix until combined. Shape into 8 rosits.

2. Insert the crisper plates in zone 1 and 2 drawers. Brush plates with oil. Place 4 rosits on each crisper plate.

3. Select Zone 1, select AIR FRY, set temperature to 175°C and set time to 13 minutes. Select MATCH. Press START/STOP to begin.

4. When time reaches 6 minutes, remove drawer from unit and flip the rostis. Reinsert drawer to continue cooking.

5. When the cooking is complete, use silicone coated tongs to remove the rostis to a serving dish and serve.

Starters & Sides

A selection of delicious starters and sides, that will complete your meals.

Honey Roasted Parsnips

Serves : 4   Prep Time : 5 Mins   Cook Time : 21 Mins

Ingredients

- 500g parsnips, peeled and chopped into chips
- 3 tbsp oil
- 2 tbsp runny honey
- ½ tsp dried thyme
- Salt and pepper to taste

Method

1. In a bowl, add parsnips, and oil. Mix until combined.

2. Insert the crisper plates in zone 1 and 2 drawers. Brush plates with oil. Place parsnips on crisper plates. Select Zone 1, select AIR FRY, set temperature to 190°C and set time to 18 minutes. Select MATCH. Press START/STOP to begin.

3. When the Zone 1 time reaches 10 minutes, remove drawers from unit and shake drawers gently. Reinsert drawer to continue cooking.

4. When cooking is complete, remove drawers from unit and add the honey, thyme, salt, pepper and shake to fully coat the parsnips. Reinsert drawer to continue cooking.

5. Select Zone 1, select AIR FRY, set temperature to 190°C and set time to 3 minutes. Select MATCH. Press START/STOP to begin.
When cooking is complete, serve immediately.

24

Potato Gratin

Serves : 6   Prep Time : 10 Mins   Cook Time : 18 Mins

Ingredients

- 3 large Maris Piper potatoes, peeled and thinly sliced
- 1 tsp garlic powder
- 250ml double cream
- 250g grated cheddar cheese
- 2 tbsp butter
- Salt and pepper to taste

Method

1. Grease the Zone 1 and 2 drawers, and layer potatoes in the drawers (ends should overlapping slightly). Season each layer with salt, garlic powder and pepper, then spread one tablespoon double cream, and finally top with a thin layer of grated cheddar. Repeat layering in two drawers. Brush the final layer with melted butter.

2. Insert drawers in the unit. Select Zone 1, select AIR FRY, set temperature to 175°C and set time to 18 minutes. Select MATCH. Press START/STOP to begin.

3. When the cooking is complete, allow to set for 5 minutes before serving.

Courgette Pizza Bites

Serves : 4   Prep Time : 10 Mins   Cook Time : 8 Mins

Ingredients

- 1 medium courgette, cut into 1/2-cm slices
- 110g pizza sauce/pizza topper
- 100g grated mozzarella cheese
- Pepperoni, cut into small pieces
- Salt and pepper to taste

Method

1. Sprinkle the courgette slices with salt and pepper.

2. Insert the crisper plates in zone 1 and 2 drawers. Brush plates with oil. Arrange the courgette slices on the plates.

3. Select Zone 1, select AIR FRY, set temperature to 175°C and set time to 4 minutes. Select MATCH. Press START/STOP to begin.

4. When the cooking is complete, use silicone coated tongs to remove the courgette and top each slice with pizza topper, cheese, and pepperoni.

5. Place the slices back in zone 1 and 2 drawers. Select Zone 1, select AIR FRY, set temperature to 175°C and set time to 4 minutes. Select MATCH. Press START/STOP to begin.
When cooking is complete, allow the courgette bites to cool slightly before serving.

Yorkshire Pudding

Serves : 12 yorkies   Prep Time : 35 Mins   Cook Time : 12 Mins

Ingredients

- 100g plain flour
- ¼ tsp salt
- 2 large eggs, room temperature
- 100ml milk
- 6 tsp sunflower oil

Method

1. In a large bowl, add flour, salt and mix. Add eggs, milk. Mix until combined and smooth. Allow to rest for 30 minutes.

2. Add 1/2 tsp of oil into 12 individual cupcake tins. Insert the crisper plates in zone 1 and 2 drawers. Place 6 cupcake tins on each crisper plate.

3. Select Zone 1, select BAKE, set temperature to 200°C and set time to 5 minutes. Select MATCH. Press START/STOP to begin.

4. When cooking is complete, remove drawers from unit and carefully fill each tin with batter ⅓ way full. Reinsert drawers to unit.

5. Select Zone 1, select BAKE, set temperature to 200°C and set time to 12 minutes. Select MATCH. Press START/STOP to begin.
When the cooking is complete, use silicone coated tongs to remove the yorkies to a serving dish and serve.

27

Cotswold Dumplings

Serves : 4   Prep Time : 10 Mins   Cook Time : 8 Mins

Ingredients

- 50g butter, softened
- 110g grated cheddar cheese
- 2 medium eggs, beaten
- 4 tsp milk
- 150g fresh (soft) breadcrumbs
- 3 tbsp dried breadcrumbs
- Salt and pepper to taste

Method

1. In a large bowl, add butter, cheese and mix until combined. Add milk, eggs, salt, pepper and whisk. Add fresh breadcrumbs, Mix and shape mixture into 16 balls, then roll in the dried breadcrumbs.

2. Insert the crisper plates in zone 1 and 2 drawers. Place 8 balls on each crisper plate. Brush balls with oil.

3. Select Zone 1, select AIR FRY, set temperature to 175°C and set time to 8 minutes. Select MATCH. Press START/STOP to begin.

4. When time reaches 4 minutes, remove drawer from unit and shake drawers. Reinsert drawer to continue cooking.

5. When the cooking is complete, use silicone coated tongs to remove the dumplings to a serving dish and serve.

Sausage Rolls

Serves : 4   Prep Time : 15 Mins   Cook Time : 20 Mins

Ingredients

- 1 onion, finely chopped
- 6 sausages, casing removed
- 1 garlic clove, minced
- 4 tbsp breadcrumbs
- 300g ready rolled puff pastry, thawed
- 1 egg mixed with 4 tbsp milk
- Sesame seeds
- Salt and pepper to taste

Method

1. In a bowl, dd sausage-meat, onion, garlic, breadcrumbs, then mix with hands until combined.

2. On a floured surface, lay pastry and cut it lengthways to 2 long rectangles. Roll the meat into sausage shapes and lay it in the center of each rectangle.

3. Brush pastry edge with egg/water mixture, then fold one side of pastry over, wrapping the filling inside. Press down with edge of a spoon to seal. Cut into pieces and brush the top with egg wash. Sprinkle with sesame seeds.

4. Insert the crisper plates in zone 1 and 2 drawers. Brush plates with oil. Place sausage rolls on crisper plate. Select Zone 1, select AIR FRY, set temperature to 180°C and set time to 18-20 minutes. Select MATCH. Press START/STOP to begin.

5. When the cooking is complete, use silicone coated tongs to remove the sausage rolls to a serving dish. Serve immediately.

29

Potato and Cheese Croquettes

Serves : 4   Prep Time : 10 Mins   Cook Time : 13 Mins

Ingredients

- 500g mashed potatoes
- 1 green onion, finely chopped
- 2 tsp chopped fresh flat leaf parsley
- 120g plain flour
- 1 large egg
- 150g breadcrumbs
- 1 tsp smoked paprika
- Salt and pepper to taste

Method

1. In another bowl, add the mashed potato, flat leaf parsley, green onion, 1 tbsp flour, salt and pepper. Mix until all combined. Form potato mixture into 2 x 5-cm logs.

2. In a bowl, add the remaining flour and season with salt, and pepper. In another bowl, add the egg, whisk. In a third bowl, add breadcrumbs, smoked paprika and mix.

3. Roll each croquette log in flour then in the beaten egg and then roll in breadcrumbs.

4. Insert the crisper plates in zone 1 and 2 drawers. Place croquettes on crisper plate and spray or brush with oil. Select Zone 1, select AIR FRY, set temperature to 190°C and set time to 12 minutes. Select MATCH. Press START/STOP to begin.

5. When the cooking is complete, use silicone coated tongs to remove the croquettes to a serving dish. Serve immediately.

Dinners & Suppers

Featuring some of UK's most popular dinner and supper recipes

Sausage and Courgette Pasta Bake

Serves : 4   **Prep Time : 5 Mins**   **Cook Time : 45 Mins**

Ingredients

- 4 English sausages, chopped
- 1 tbsp oil
- 1 medium onion, finely chopped
- 2 garlic cloves, minced
- 250g penne pasta
- 1 (400g) tin chopped tomatoes
- 1 medium courgette, grated and squeezed to remove excess water
- 4 tbsp breadcrumbs
- 100g grated Cheddar
- 1 tsp dried oregano
- 500ml chicken stock
- Salt and pepper to taste

Method

1. With no crisping plate installed, add all ingredients to Zone 1 and 2 drawers (divide the amount between the two drawers). Stir to combine. Cover with tin foil (crimp the foil tightly around the edges of the drawer so that no steam can escape). Insert drawers into the unit.

2. Select zone 1, select BAKE, set temperature to 195°C, and set time to 45 minutes. Select MATCH. Press the START/STOP button to begin cooking.

3. When time reaches 35 minutes, remove tin foil and stir. Reinsert drawers to continue cooking. When cooking is complete, stir then serve.

Mozzarella Stuffed Meatballs and Rice

Serves : 4   Prep Time : 10 Mins   Cook Time : 35 Mins

Ingredients

- 500g minced beef
- 75g breadcrumbs
- 2 tbsp grated parmigiano reggiano
- 1 large egg
- 2 garlic cloves, minced
- 1 tsp dried oregano
- 180g long grain rice
- 360ml chicken or vegetable stock
- Salt and pepper to taste
- 300g tin chopped tomato
- 2 garlic cloves, minced
- ¼ tsp dried oregano

Method

1. In a bowl, add minced beef, breadcrumbs, cheese, egg, garlic, oregano, salt and pepper. Mix until combined.

2. Form the meatballs with two tablespoons of the beef mixture for each ball.

3. Install a crisping plate in the Zone 1 drawer, then place meatballs in the drawer and insert drawer in unit.

4. With no crisping plate installed, place rice, stock, salt and pepper in the Zone 2 drawer and stir to combine.

5. Select Zone 1, select AIR FRY, set temperature to 185°C, and set time to 17 minutes. Select Zone 2, select BAKE, set temperature to 200°C and set time for 35 minutes. Select SYNC. Press the START/PAUSE button to begin cooking.

6. When the Zone 1 time reaches 15 minutes, remove drawer from unit and add the chopped tomatoes, garlic, oregano, salt, pepper and stir gently. Reinsert drawer to continue cooking. When the cooking is complete, serve meatballs with rice.

33

Rosemary Garlic Lamb Chops

Serves : 4   Prep Time : 25 Mins   Cook Time : 12 Mins

Ingredients

- 600g lamb chops
- 2 tbsp oil
- 3 rosemary sprigs
- 2 thyme sprigs
- 3 cloves cloves, minced
- Salt and pepper to taste

Method

1. In a bowl, add oil, rosemary, thyme, garlic, salt, and pepper. Mix until all lamb chops coated with seasoning. Set aside for 15 minutes.

2. Insert crisper plates in zone 1 and 2 drawers. Brush with oil. Place the lamb chops in an even layer into each drawer. Insert drawers in unit. Select zone 1, select AIR FRY, set temperature to 200°C and set time to 12 minutes. Select MATCH. Press START/STOP to begin. (When time reaches 6 minutes, remove drawers from unit and flip the chops. Reinsert drawers to continue cooking).

3. When cooking is complete, remove both drawers from the unit and remove the lamb chops from and allow to rest for 5 minutes before serving.

Sausage and Peppers

Serves : 6   Prep Time : 5 Mins   Cook Time : 19 Mins

Ingredients

- 3 bell peppers , sliced
- 1 large onion, sliced
- 1 tbsp oil
- 6 sausages
- Salt and pepper to taste
- 6 of your favourite buns

Method

1. In a bowl, add all ingredients (except buns) and mix.

2. Insert crisper plates in zone 1 and 2 drawers. Divide the sausage mixture into each drawer. Insert drawers in unit. Select zone 1, select AIR FRY, set temperature to 200°C and set time to 16 minutes. Select MATCH. Press START/STOP to begin. (When time reaches 8 minutes, remove drawers from unit and shake drawers. Reinsert drawers to continue cooking).

3. When cooking is complete, remove drawers from unit. Divide the onion and peppers between the buns, then place one sausages in each bun and serve

Sausage and Peppers

It's delicious on its own or as a quick addition to pasta, sandwiches, and other dishes.

Lamb Burgers

Serves : 4   Prep Time : 5 Mins   Cook Time : 12 Mins

Ingredients

- 500g lamb mince
- 2 garlic cloves, minced
- 1 onion, grated
- 2 tbsp chopped mint leaves
- Salt and pepper to taste

Method

1. In a large bowl, add all ingredients and mix until combined.

2. Divide mixture into 4 equal portions. Roll each portion into a ball and then flatten it.

3. Add the burgers in a single layer in zone 1 & 2 drawers (with crisper plate inserted), then insert drawers in unit. Select zone 1, select Air Fry, set temperature to 180°C and set time to 12 minutes. Select MATCH. Press START/STOP to begin.

4. When time reaches 6 minutes, remove drawers from unit and flip the burgers. Reinsert drawers to continue cooking.

5. When cooking is complete, let the burgers rest for 2 minutes before serving.

Beef Short Ribs

Serves : 4   Prep Time : 30 Mins   Cook Time : 13 Mins

Ingredients

- 600g beef short ribs
- ½ tsp onion powder
- 2 tbsp dark soy sauce
- 2 tbsp oil
- 2 garlic cloves, minced
- 3 tsp grated ginger
- ½ tsp ground black pepper
- 1 tbsp brown sugar

Method

1. In a bowl, add all ingredients and mix until ribs coated with seasoning. Leave ribs in the marinade for 30 mins.

2. Add the short ribs in a single layer in zone 1 & 2 drawers (with crisper plate inserted), then insert drawers in unit. Select zone 1, select ROAST, set temperature to 200°C and set time to 13 minutes, Select MATCH. Press START/STOP to begin.

3. When time reaches 5 minutes, remove drawers from unit and flip the short ribs. Reinsert drawers to continue cooking.
When cooking is complete, remove drawers and serve.

Popeseye Steak with Garlic Dill Butter

🔔 Serves : 4   🍝 Prep Time : 10 Mins   🍲 Cook Time : 15 Mins

Ingredients

For the dill butter

- 2 tbsp butter, softened
- 2 tbsp dill, finely chopped
- 1 garlic clove, minced

For the Popeseye steak

- 4 (150g each) Popeseye steaks, room temperature
- 2 tsp oil
- 2 tbsp butter, softened
- Salt and pepper to taste

Method

1. In a small bowl, add butter and mash with a fork. Add the minced garlic, dill and mix.

2. Transfer the garlic dill butter on a piece of cling film. Form it into a sausage shape and twist the ends to seal. Place in the refrigerator.

3. Pat dry the steaks with kitchen paper. Rub steaks with butter and season both sides with salt and pepper.

4. Place the steaks in Zone 1 and 2 drawers (with crisper plate inserted), then insert drawers in unit. Select zone 1 , Select AIR FRY, set temperature to 200°C and set time to 15 minutes. Select MATCH. Press START/STOP to begin.

5. When time reaches 7 minutes, remove drawers from unit and flip the short ribs. Reinsert drawers to continue cooking.
When cooking is complete, transfer the steak to a plate, top with garlic dill butter, cover with tin foil and rest for 5 mins. Serve.

39

Barnsley Chops

🔔 **Serves : 4**   🥣 **Prep Time : 40 Mins**   🍲 **Cook Time : 15 Mins**

Ingredients

- 2 (350g each) Barnsley/saddle chops
- 2 tbsp oil
- Salt and pepper to taste
- 2 tsp chopped rosemary
- 2 tsp butter

Method

1. In a shallow dish rub chops with oil and then sprinkle with the chopped rosemary. Cover and refrigerate for 30 mins

2. Remove the chops out of the refrigerator and set aside until reaches room temperature. Sprinkle the chops with salt and pepper.

3. Place the chops in Zone 1 and 2 drawers (with crisper plate inserted), then insert drawers in unit. Select Zone, Select AIR FRY, set temperature to 200°C and set time to 15 minutes. Select MATCH. Press START/STOP to begin.

4. When cooking is complete, transfer chops to a plate and top with butter and loosely cover with tin foil for 5 minutes before serving.

Mustard Glazed Tomahawk Steak with Garlic and Parsley Sauce

Serves : 4   Prep Time : 10 Mins   Cook Time : 25 Mins

Ingredients

- 1 kg Tomahawk steak, room temperature
- 2 tbsp butter
- Salt and pepper to taste
- 1 tbsp wholegrain mustard

For the sauce:

- 1 tbsp Balsamic Vinegar
- Juice and zest of 1 lemon
- 3 garlic cloves, minced
- 1 Punch fresh flat leaf parsley, finely chopped
- 120ml olive oil
- Salt and pepper to taste

Method

1. Season steak on both sides with salt and pepper.

2. Place the steak in zone 1 drawer (with crisper plate inserted), then insert drawer in unit. Select zone 1, select ROAST, set temperature to 190°C and set time to 15 minutes. (For medium rare: cook for 15 mins . For rare: cook for 12 mins).

3. When time reaches 7 minutes, remove drawers from unit and flip the steaks. Reinsert drawers to continue cooking.

4. When cooking is complete, remove drawer and brush steak with mustard. Reinsert drawers. Select ROAST, set temp to 190°C and set time to 10 min. Press START/ STOP button to begin cooking.

5. Remove drawer, remove steak, transfer to a plate and top with butter. Loosely cover the steak with foil in a warm place, for 5 minutes.

6. In a bowl, add all sauce ingredients and mix until combined. Slice steak and serve with sauce.

Stuffed Saddle of Lamb

Serves : 4   Prep Time : 15 Mins   Cook Time : 1 hr 20 mins

Ingredients

- 1 kg boneless saddle or leg of lamb, room temperature
- 2 onions, cut into thick slices
- 1 tsp oil
- Salt and pepper to taste
- 2 tbsp oil

For the stuffing

- 1 tbsp thyme, finely chopped
- 2 garlic cloves, minced
- 1 tbsp parsley, finely chopped
- 1 tbsp rosemary, finely chopped
- zest and juice of 1 lemon
- 100g breadcrumbs
- 1 handful pine nuts
- Salt and pepper to taste

Method

1. In a large mixing bowl, add all the stuffing ingredients and mix until combined.

2. Place the saddle of lamb skin side down on a cutting board. Scoop the stuffing into the middle of the saddle.

3. Cut 4 pieces of string about 15-cm longer than the saddle of lamb. Roll up the lamb and tie with the strings.

4. Insert the crisper plates in Zone 1 drawer. Place onion on crisper plate. Then Put lamb on top of onions and rub with oil. Season with salt and pepper.

5. Select Zone 1, select ROAST, set temperature to 195°C and set time to 20 minutes. Press START/STOP to begin.

6. When time reaches 20 minutes in Zine 1 drawer, turn the heat down to 180°C and Continue to ROAST for 1 hour.

7. When cooking is complete, remove lamb from the unit. Loosely cover with tin foil in a warm place, for 20 minutes. Slice and serve.

Stuffed Saddle of Lamb

This Stuffed Leg of Lamb dish is a fantastic holiday supper that is much easier to prepare than it appears!

Beef Bites and Gravy

Serves : 4-6   Prep Time : 5 Mins   Cook Time : 30 mins

Ingredients

- 1 kg diced beef, cut into small cubes
- 2 tbsp oil
- 1 onion, finely chopped
- 2 garlic cloves, minced
- 225g mushroom, sliced
- 500ml beef stock
- 2 tbsp Worcestershire sauce
- 1 bay leaf
- 1 tbsp tomato paste
- Salt and pepper to taste

To Thicken Gravy:
- 1 tbsp cornflour mixed with 1 tbsp water

Method

1. With no crisping plate installed, place all ingredients (except cornflour/water mixture) in the Zone 1 drawer. Stir to combine.

2. Select Zone 1, select AIR FRY, set temperature to 200°C, and set time to 30 minutes. Press the START/PAUSE button to begin cooking.

3. When time reaches 15 minutes, remove drawers from unit and stir. Reinsert drawers to continue cooking.

4. When the cooking is complete, remove drawers and stir, add the cornflour/water mixture and stir until thickened .
Serve with pasta, rice or potato mash.

Scotch Eggs

🍽 Serves : 8   🥘 Prep Time : 15 Mins   🍲 Cook Time : 13 mins

Ingredients

- 6 eggs, boiled and peeled
- 400g Sausagemeat or 400g sausage, casing removed
- 4 tbsp plain flour
- 1/2 tsp garlic powder
- 1 large egg beaten
- 120 g breadcrumbs
- 1/2 smoked paprika
- Salt and pepper to taste

Method

1. In a bowl, add the flour and season with salt, pepper and garlic powder. In another bowl, add the beaten egg. In a third bowl, add breadcrumbs, smoked paprika and mix.

2. Divide the sausage into 6 equal balls. On a working surface lined with baking paper, then pat the balls enough to wrap an egg.

3. Place one egg in the centre of each sausagement and wrap it around the egg. Roll each covered egg in flour then in the beaten egg and then roll in breadcrumbs.

4. Insert the crisper plates in zone 1 and 2 drawers. Place Scotch eggs on crisper plate and spray or brush with oil. Select AIR FRY, set temperature to 190°C and set time to 13 minutes. Select MATCH. Press START/STOP to begin.

5. When the cooking is complete, use silicone coated tongs to remove the scotch eggs to a serving dish. Serve with a salad, and chips.

Shepherd's Pie

Serves : 4   Prep Time : 10 Mins   Cook Time : 25 mins

Ingredients

Topping:
- 400g leftover mashed potatoes
- 60ml milk
- 3 tbsp melted butter
- 100g grated cheddar cheese

Filling:
- 1 onion, chopped
- 2 garlic cloves, minced
- 450g minced beef
- 150g frozen garden peas and carrots
- 2 tsp Worcestershire sauce
- ½ tsp dried thyme leaves
- Salt and pepper to taste

Method

1. In a bowl, add all topping ingredients, season with salt, pepper. Mix until combined, set aside.

2. With no crisping plate installed, place all the filling ingredients in the Zone 1 drawer, season with salt and peeper. Stir to combine.

3. Select Zone 1, select AIR FRY, set temperature to 200°C, and set time to 12 minutes. Press the START/PAUSE button to begin cooking.

4. When time reaches 6 minutes, remove drawers from unit and stir. Reinsert drawers to continue cooking.

5. When cooking is complete, remove drawer from unit and drain any fat.

6. Divide the beef mixture into the zone 1 and 2 drawers. Top with the potato mash mixture. Insert both drawers into unit.

7. Select Zone 1, select BAKE, set temperature to 190°C and set time to 13 minutes. Select MATCH. Press START/STOP to begin.
To serve, divide the pie between four plates.

Mini Beef Wellingtons

Serves : 8   Prep Time : 13 Mins   Cook Time : 20 mins

Ingredients

- 450g rump steaks, trimmed and cut into 5-cm cubes
- 1 tbsp oil
- 320g frozen puff pastry sheets, thawed
- 3 tbsp Dijon mustard
- 150g chopped and cooked mushroom
- 1 egg, lightly beaten
- Salt and pepper to taste

Method

1. Season the steak cubes with salt and pepper and coat with oil.

2. Place the steaks in zone 1 and 2 drawers (with crisper plate inserted), then insert drawers in unit. Select ROAST, set temperature to 190°C and set time to 6 minutes. Select MATCH. Press START/STOP to begin.

3. When the cooking is complete, transfer the steak cubes to a plate. Set aside.

4. On a lightly floured surface, lay the pastry sheet and cut vertically into three equal strips. Cut each strip into 5 squares.

5. Spread some of the mushroom and mustard on each pastry square, then place a piece on top of each mushroom-covered squares.

6. Wrap the pastry around each beef piece, sealing the edges and brush all over with the beaten egg.

7. Place the mini beef wellingtons in zone 1 and 2 drawers (with crisper plate inserted), then insert drawers in unit. Select AIR FRY, set temperature to 190°C and set time to 7 minutes. Select MATCH. Press START/STOP to begin cooking.

8. When the cooking is complete, transfer the mini beef wellingtons into a serving plate and serve.

Mini Beef Wellingtons

Ideal for a Sunday lunch. Served with fluffy potato mash.

Toad In The Hole

Serves : 4-6   Prep Time : 10 Mins   Cook Time : 35 mins

Ingredients

- 60g plain flour
- 4 eggs
- 240g whole milk
- 1 tbsp English mustard
- 2 tbsp oil or melted butter
- 8 small English sausages
- Salt and pepper to taste

Method

1. In a bowl, add flour, salt and pepper. Add the eggs and milk and mix until combined and smooth.

2. (If it's too thick, add more milk). Cover and set aside.

3. With no crisping plate installed, place the sausages in zone 1 and 2 drawers, add 1 tbsp butter or oil in each drawer, then insert drawers in unit. Select AIR FRY, set temperature to 200°C and set time to 10 minutes. Select MATCH. Press START/STOP to begin cooking.

4. When cooking is complete, remove drawer from unit and carefully pour in the batter on top of the oil and sausages. Insert both drawers into unit.

5. Select Zone 1, select BAKE, set temperature to 180°C and set time to 20 minutes. Select MATCH. Press START/STOP to begin cooking.
When cooking is complete, transfer into plates and serve.

Forfar Bridie

Serves : 6   Prep Time : 40 Mins   Cook Time : 40 mins

Ingredients

For the shortcrust pastry:

- 450g plain flour
- 225g cold unsalted butter, cut into small cubes
- Pinch of salt
- Cold water

For the filling:

- 450g beef skirt steak, cut into 1-cm cubes
- 1 onion, finely chopped
- 1/2 tsp dry mustard powder
- 1 tbsp plain flour
- Salt and pepper to taste
- 1 egg, beaten

Method

1. In a bowl, add filling ingredients, mix and set aside.

2. In a large bowl, add flour, salt. Mix until combined. Add the butter, and rub with hands into the flour until mixture resembles breadcrumbs. Add water gradually while kneading until a dough comes together (Do Not over knead). Shape into a ball, cover with cling film and refrigerate for 30 Minutes.

3. Divide pastry into 6 balls. Transfer into a floured surface, then roll out each ball into 15-cm circle.

4. Fill each pastry circle with filling mixture on one side of each circle and brush edges with beaten egg. Fold top half of the pasty down over the filling and seal around the edges. Brush tops with egg.

5. Insert a crisper plate in both drawers. Place 3 Bridies in each drawer, then insert drawers in unit.

6. Select Zone 1, select AIR FRY, set temperature to 150°C, and set time to 40 minutes. Select MATCH. Press the START/PAUSE button to begin cooking. (If they start to get too brown, cover with tin foil).

7. When cooking is complete, transfer to a plate. let cool for 10 minutes before serving.

50

Roasted Leg of Lamb and Potatoes

Serves : 4   Prep Time : 10 Mins   Cook Time : 25 mins

Ingredients

- 750g lamb leg
- 4 tbs oil
- 600g Maris Piper or King Edwards potatoes, peeled and cut into cubes or quarters
- 1 tbsp garlic powder
- 1 tbsp smoked paprika
- 1 tbsp dried thyme
- 1 tbsp dried rosemary
- Salt and pepper to taste

Method

1. Soak cut potatoes in cold water for 30 minutes to remove excess starch. Drain, then pat with a paper towel until very dry.

2. Season the potatoes, garlic powder, smoked paprika, thyme, 2 tbsp oil, salt and pepper. Mix until all potatoes coated with seasoning.

3. Rub the lamb leg with 2 tbsp oil, rosemary, season with salt and pepper.

4. Insert a crisper plate in both drawers. Place lamb leg in zone 1 drawer, then insert drawer in unit. Place potatoes in zone 2 drawer, then insert drawer in unit.

5. Select zone 1, select ROAST, set temperature to 180°C and set time to 25 minute. Select zone 2, select AIR FRY, set temperature to 200°C, and set time to 25 minutes. Select START/STOP to begin.

6. When Zone 2 time reaches 10 minutes, remove drawer from unit and shake drawer. Reinsert drawer to continue cooking.

7. When cooking is complete, remove the lamb and let it rest before slicing. (The lamb is cooked when its internal temperature reaches 63°C). Serve lamb with potato.

Haggis Burger

🛎 Serves : 6   🍲 Prep Time : 5 Mins   🍲 Cook Time : 8 mins

Ingredients

- 300g haggis
- 300g beef mince
- 120g grated cheddar
- Salt and pepper to taste

Method

1. In a bowl add all ingredients and mix with hand until combined. Divide mixture into 6 portions. Roll and press together, then flatten slightly.

2. Insert a crisper plate in both drawers. Place burgers in Zone 1 and Zone 2 drawers, then insert drawers in unit.

3. Select zone 1, select AIR FRY, set temperature to 190°C and set time to 8 minute. Select MATCH. Select START/STOP to begin.

4. When Zone 1 time reaches 4 minutes, remove drawer from unit and flip burgers. Reinsert drawer to continue cooking.

5. When cooking is complete, remove from unit. Serve with with your favourite toppings (lettuce, tomato, and sauces you like).

Minced Beef and Cheddar Casserole

🛎 Serves : 4   🍳 Prep Time : 5 Mins   ⏲ Cook Time : 27 mins

Ingredients

- 450 minced beef
- 2 tbs oil
- 1 large onion, chopped
- 3 garlic cloves, minced
- 350g tomato sauce
- 1 small carrot, peeled and finely chopped
- 300g cooked rice
- 1 celery stalk, thinly sliced
- 60g grated cheddar cheese
- 60g grated mozzarella
- Salt and pepper to taste

Method

1. With no crisping plate installed, place minced beef, onion, garlic, carrot, celery in the Zone 1 drawer, season with salt and peeper. Stir to combine.

2. Select Zone 1, select AIR FRY, set temperature to 200°C, and set time to 12 minutes. Press the START/PAUSE button to begin cooking

3. When time reaches 6 minutes, remove drawer from unit and stir. Reinsert drawer to continue cooking.

4. When cooking is complete, remove drawer from unit and drain any fat.

5. Divide the beef mixture into the zone 1 and 2 drawers. Top with the rice, tomato sauce, salt and pepper, stir gently. Sprinkle with cheddar and mozzarella. Insert both drawers into unit.

6. Select zone 1, select BAKE, set temperature to 200°C and set time to 15 minutes. Select MATCH. Press START/STOP to begin.
When cooking is complete, serve.

Minced Beef and Cheddar Casserole

super easy to throw together! It's comforting and uses simple ingredients.

Lemon Garlic Chicken and Orzo

Serves : 4   Prep Time : 5 Mins   Cook Time : 30 mins

Ingredients

- 4 bone-in, skin-on chicken thighs
- 2 tbsp oil
- 1 tsp garlic powder
- 1 small onion, finely chopped
- 2 tbsp butter
- 225g dry orzo pasta
- 100g fresh spinach
- 2 garlic cloves, finely chopped
- 700ml chicken stock
- 50ml double cream
- Salt and pepper to taste

Method

1. Pat the chicken dry, season with salt and pepper and garlic powder.

2. Install a crisping plate in the Zone 1 drawer, then place chicken thighs in the drawer and insert drawer in unit.

3. With no crisping plate installed, place orzo, stock, spinach garlic, butter and onions in the Zone 2 drawer and stir to combine.

4. Select Zone 1, select AIR FRY, set temperature to 200°C, and set time to 26 minutes. Select Zone 2, select BAKE, set temperature to 200°C and set time for 30 minutes. Select SYNC. Press the START/PAUSE button to begin cooking.

5. When cooking is complete, cover orzo with foil and leave to rest for 5 mins before serving. Serve chicken with orzo.

Chicken Pasties

🔔 Serves : 8   🥣 Prep Time : 20 Mins   🍲 Cook Time : 25 mins

Ingredients

Pasties

- 500g plain flour
- 250g cold butter, cubed
- 1 egg , beaten for brushing
- Cold water, as needed

Filling

- 1 turnip, finely chopped
- 1 onion, , finely chopped
- 1 carrot, finely chopped
- 1 celery stalk, finely chopped
- 2 boneless and skinless chicken breasts, cut into 1-cm cubes
- 60g plain flour
- 120g grated cheddar cheese
- 60ml melted butter
- Salt & pepper to taste
- 1 egg mixed with 1 tbsp water

Method

1. In a bowl, add filling ingredients, mix and set aside.

2. In a large bowl, add flour, salt. Mix until combined. Add the butter, and rub with hands into flour until resembles breadcrumbs. Add water gradually while kneading until a dough comes together (Do Not over knead).

3. Divide dough into 8 balls. Transfer into a floured surface, then roll out each ball into 20-cm circle.

4. Fill each pastie with filling mixture on one side of each pastry circle and brush edges with beaten egg. Fold top half of the pasty down over the filling and seal around the edges. Brush tops with egg.

5. Insert a crisper plate in both drawers. Place 4 chicken pasties in each drawer, then insert drawers in unit.

6. Select Zone 1, select AIR FRY, set temperature to 170°C, and set time to 30-35 minutes. Select MATCH. Press the START/PAUSE button to begin cooking

7. When time reaches 15 minutes, remove drawer from unit and flip the pasties. Reinsert drawer to continue cooking.
When cooking is complete, let cool for 5 minutes before serving.

56

Stuffed Chicken Breast

Serves : 4   Prep Time : 10 Mins   Cook Time : 25 mins

Ingredients

- 4 medium, boneless and skinless chicken breasts
- 1 tbsp smoked paprika
- 1 tsp dried thyme
- 1 tbsp onion powder
- 60g pepperoni slices
- 150g mozzarella slices
- 100g grated cheddar
- Salt and pepper to taste

Method

1. Make a slit in each chicken breast using a sharp knife. Season outside of the chicken breasts with paprika, thyme, onion powder, salt and pepper.

2. Stuff each chicken breast with ¼ of the pepperoni slices, ¼ of the cheddar and 2 mozzarella slices (Use toothpicks to secure the stuffing if needed).

3. Insert a crisper plate in both drawers. Place two chicken breasts in each drawer, sprinkle with oil, then insert drawers in unit.

4. Select Zone 1, select AIR FRY, set temperature to 180°C, and set time to 25-30 minutes. Select MATCH. Press the START/PAUSE button to begin cooking (The internal temperature of the chicken needs to reach 74°C to ensure that it's cooked).

5. When cooking is complete, let the chicken rest for 5 minutes before serving.

Devilled Chicken

Serves : 4   Prep Time : 5 Mins   Cook Time : 18 mins

Ingredients

- 4 boneless chicken thighs

For the Marinade:

- ½ tsp red chilli
- 1 tsp mustard powder
- 1 garlic clove, minced
- 3 tbsp tomato sauce
- 1 tbsp grated fresh ginger
- 2 tsp Worcestershire sauce
- 1 tbsp oil
- Salt and pepper to taste

Method

1. In a large bowl, add all marinade ingredients and mix until combined. Place the chicken thighs into the bowl and cover with marinade.

2. Cover the bowl with cling film and refrigerate for an hour.

3. Add the chicken thighs in a single layer in Zone 1 and Zone 2 drawers (with crisper plate inserted), then insert drawers in unit. Select zone 1, select ROAST, set temperature at 190°C for 14-18 mins (depending on the size of the thighs), Select MATCH. Press the START/PAUSE button to begin cooking.
Serve with baked potato and salad.

Chicken and Potatoes

Serves : 3   Prep Time : 5 Mins   Cook Time : 18 mins

Ingredients

- 3 medium potatoes, peeled and cut into 2 1/2-cm cubes
- 3 chicken breasts/thighs diced into 5-cm pieces
- 4 garlic cloves, minced
- 2 tsp smoked paprika
- 1 tsp thyme
- 2 tbsp oil
- Salt and pepper to taste

Method

1. In a bowl, add potatoes, 1/4 of the garlic, and half of the seasonings and 1 tbsp oil. Mix.

2. Insert crisper plate into both drawers. Place potatoes in zone 2 drawer, then insert drawer in unit.

3. In the same bowl, add chicken, remaining garlic, seasoning and oil. Mix. Place chicken in zone 1 drawer, then insert drawer in unit.

4. Select zone 1, select ROAST, set temperature to 200°C, and set time to 10 minutes. Select zone 2, select AIR FRY, set temperature to 200°C and set time to 18 minutes. Select SYNC. Press the START/STOP button to begin cooking.

5. When zone 1 time reaches 5 minutes, remove drawer, flip chicken using silicone-tipped tongs. Reinsert drawer to continue cooking.

6. When zone 2 time reaches 10 minutes, remove drawer from unit and shake drawer for 10 seconds. Reinsert drawer to continue cooking. When cooking is complete, serve chicken with potatoes.

Chicken Parmesan

🍽 Serves : 2   Prep Time : 15 Mins   Cook Time : 40 mins

Ingredients

- 2 tbsp plain flour
- 40g breadcrumbs
- 2 tbsp fresh Parmesan cheese, finely grated
- 1 egg, beaten
- 2 skinless chicken breasts
- 4 tbsp pizza sauce/pizza topper
- 50g mozzarella slices

Method

1. Bash the chicken breasts with a rolling pin until 1-cm in thickness.

2. In a bowl, add flour, salt, pepper and mix. In another bowl, add eggs and whisk. In a third bowl, add bread crumbs and Parmesan.

3. Coat each chicken breast with flour, then dip into egg, then coat in breadcrumbs.

4. Insert a crisper plate into both drawers. Place chicken in Zone 1 and 2 drawers, then insert drawers in unit.

5. Select zone 1, select AIR FRY, set temperature to 200°C, and set time to 15 minutes. Select MATCH. Press the START/STOP button to begin cooking.

6. When Zone 1 time reaches 8 minutes, remove drawers from unit and turn the chicken using silicone-tipped tongs. Reinsert drawers to continue cooking.

7. When cooking is complete, remove drawers from unit and top chicken with pizza sauce and mozzarella. Continue to AIR FRY at 200°C for 5 min.
Serve with salad and chips or pasta.

Garlic Chicken Wings and Cheesy Pasta

🛎️ Serves : 4   🥣 Prep Time : 10 Mins   🍲 Cook Time : 21 mins

Ingredients

Chicken wings

- 1kg chicken wings
- 2 tbsp cornflour
- 2 tsp smoked paprika
- 2 tsp garlic powder
- Salt and pepper to taste

Cheesy pasta

- 225g dried spirali pasta
- 120ml double cream
- 450ml whole milk
- 200g mature cheddar cheese, divided
- 2 tbsp butter
- ¼ tsp garlic powder
- ¼ tsp onion powder
- Salt and pepper to taste

Method

1. In a bowl, add chicken wings, cornflour, seasoning and mix.

2. Insert a crisper plate into Zone 1 drawer. Place chicken wings in Zone 1 drawer, then insert drawer in unit.

3. With no crisping plate installed, grease Zone 2 drawer, add all pasta ingredients (except butter). Stir. Insert drawer into the unit.

4. Select Zone 1, select AIR FRY, set temperature to 200°C, and set time to 20 minutes. Select Zone 2, select BAKE, set temperature to 175°C and set time for 21 minutes. Select SYNC. Press the START/PAUSE button to begin cooking.

5. When the Zone 2 time reaches 11 minutes, remove drawer from unit and stir gently. Reinsert drawer to continue cooking.

6. When cooking is complete, remove drawers from unit and top the pasta with chicken wings and serve.

61

Chicken and Rice Casserole

Serves : 4   Prep Time : 5 Mins   Cook Time : 45 mins

Ingredients

- 2 large boneless, skinless chicken breast, cut into bite size pieces
- 1 tbsp oil
- 500ml chicken stock
- 150g uncooked long grain white rice
- 1/2 tsp onion powder
- 100g frozen carrots, sweetcorn and peas
- 1 bell pepper, finely chopped
- 100g runner beans, chopped
- 50g grated cheddar cheese

Method

1. With no crisping plate installed, add rice, stock, frozen carrots, corn, beans, peas, bell pepper, oil, onion powder, salt, and pepper to Zone 1 and 2 drawers (divide the amount between the two drawers). Stir to combine. Cover with tin foil. Insert drawers into the unit.

2. Select zone 1, select BAKE, set temperature to 180°C, and set time to 45 minutes. Select MATCH. Press the START/STOP button to begin cooking.

3. When cooking is complete, remove drawers from unit and stir in the cheese, let sit for 5 minutes, then serve.

Chicken and Rice Casserole

Dinner doesn't get much easier or more delicious than this cheesy Chicken and Rice Casserole, which only takes less than 5 minutes to prepare.

Baked Chicken And Gravy

Serves : 5   Prep Time : 5 Mins   Cook Time : 30 mins

Ingredients

For The Chicken:

- 1 1/4 kg bone in, skin on chicken thighs
- 2 tsp oil
- 1 tsp smoked paprika
- 1 tsp dried thyme
- 1 tsp garlic powder

For The Gravy:

- 4 tbsp plain flour
- 400ml beef stock
- Salt & pepper to taste

Method

1. In a bowl, add chicken, oil, paprika, thyme, garlic powder, salt and pepper. Mix until chicken coated all over with spices. Set aside.

2. In a bowl, add gravy ingredients and whisk until combined.

3. With no crisping plate installed, Place the chicken into Zone 1 and 2 drawers. Pour the gravy evenly into drawers around the chicken.

4. Select zone 1, select BAKE, set temperature to 190°C, and set time to 30 minutes. Select MATCH. Press the START/STOP button to begin cooking.

5. When cooking is complete, remove chicken onto a plate, then whisk the gravy until smooth. Serve gravy with chicken.

Butter Chicken and Rice

Serves : 4   Prep Time : 5 Mins   Cook Time : 33 mins

Ingredients

Butter chicken:

- 1 kg boneless, skinless chicken thighs, cut into cubes
- 1 (400g) tin chopped tomato
- 20g butter, melted
- 240ml double cream
- 1 large onion, finely chopped
- 3 garlic cloves, minced
- 1 tbsp garam marsala
- ½ tsp cumin
- 1/4 tsp cinnamon
- 1 tbsp grated fresh ginger
- Salt and pepper to taste

Rice:

- 170g long grain or basmati rice, rinsed and drained
- 340ml water
- 2 tsp oil
- Salt to taste

Method

1. In a bowl, add all butter chicken ingredients (except chicken) and whisk until combined. Add the chicken into this mixture and mix until coated with spices.

2. With no crisping plate installed, Place the chicken into Zone 1 drawer. Pour the sauce over the chicken. Insert drawer into the unit.

3. With no crisping plate installed, add rice, water, oil, salt, and pepper to Zone 2 drawer. Stir to combine. Insert drawer into the unit.

4. Select Zone 1, select AIR FRY, set temperature to 180°C, and set time to 30 minutes. Select Zone 2, select BAKE, set temperature to 200°C and set time for 33 minutes. Select SYNC. Press the START/PAUSE button to begin cooking.
When cooking is complete, serve butter chicken with rice.

Chicken And Dumplings Casserole

Serves : 5   Prep Time : 15 Mins   Cook Time : 45 mins

Ingredients

- 850ml chicken stock
- 1 kg chicken breasts, cut into bite-size pieces
- 1 large onion, finely chopped
- 200g potatoes, peeled and finely chopped
- 2 celery stalks, finely chopped
- 3 tbsp tomato paste
- 3 carrots, peeled, thinly sliced
- 1 tsp dried thyme
- 80g plain flour
- Salt & pepper to taste

For the dumpling

- 170g self-raising flour
- 100g frozen butter, grated
- Pinch of salt
- Cold water, as needed

Method

1. In a bowl, whisk together 80g plain flour and the chicken stock, until combined and smooth. Season with salt and pepper.

2. With no crisping plate installed, add onion, celery, potatoes, carrot, thyme, tomato paste, chicken. Pour over the flour/stock mixture into Zone 1 drawer and stir. Insert drawer in unit.

3. Select Zone 1, select AIR FRY, set temperature to 170°C, and set time to 45 minutes. Press the START/PAUSE button to begin cooking.

4. In a bowl, add flour, butter, and salt. Mix until mixture resembles breadcrumbs. Add water gradually while mixing, until dough holds together. Don't over mix. Divide into 8 balls.

5. When time reaches 30 Minutes, remove drawer and place the balls on top of chicken. Reinsert drawer to continue cooking.
When cooking is complete, serve chicken with dumplings.

66

Chicken Fajitas Bowls

Serves : 4   Prep Time : 5 Mins   Cook Time : 30 mins

Ingredients

Chicken Fajitas:

- Juice of one lemon, divided
- 2 tbsp oil
- 700g boneless, skinless chicken thighs or breasts, cut into strips
- 1 tsp garlic powder
- 1 tsp onion powder
- 1 tsp smoked paprika
- ½ tsp ground cumin
- 1 medium onion, sliced
- 1 of each (yellow, red and green bell peppers), sliced

Rice:

- 200g uncooked long grain rice
- 1 tbsp oil
- 1 tbsp tomato paste
- 1 garlic clove, minced
- 500ml chicken or vegetable stock
- Salt and pepper to taste

Method

1. In a bowl, add all chicken fajitas and mix until all coated with seasoning and oil.

2. Install a crisping plate in the Zone 1 drawer, then chicken/pepper mixture in the drawer and insert drawer in unit.

3. With no crisping plate installed, place rice, stock, tomato paste, oil, salt and pepper in the Zone 2 drawer and stir to combine.

4. Select Zone 1, select AIR FRY, set temperature to 190°C, and set time to 15 minutes. Select Zone 2, select BAKE, set temperature to 200°C and set time for 30 minutes. Select SYNC. Press the START/PAUSE button to begin cooking.

5. When the Zone 1 time reaches 10 minutes, remove basket from unit and stir chicken using silicone-tipped tongs. Reinsert basket to continue cooking.
When cooking is complete, mix chicken fajitas with rice and serve.

Baked Salmon with Lemon and Butter

🔔 Serves : 4   🥣 Prep Time : 10 Mins   🍲 Cook Time : 20 mins

Ingredients

- 1 kg side of salmon, skin on, room temperature
- 2 garlic cloves, minced
- 2 lemons, sliced
- Juice and zest of 1 lemon
- 5 springs fresh rosemary, roughly chopped
- Salt and pepper to taste
- 2 tbsp butter, melted

Method

1. Line a chopping board with enough tin foil to cover the salmon. Lightly grease the tin foil.

2. Scatter some chopped rosemary over the foil, then lay the salmon on top. Brush the salmon top with the melted butter and lemon juice. Season the salt and pepper.

3. Arrange the lemon slices over the top then sprinkle over with remaining chopped rosemary, minced garlic and lemon zest. Fold the sides of the tin foil up and over the top of the salmon until it is completely covered.

4. Insert a crisper plate into Zone 1 drawer. Place salmon in drawer, then insert drawer in unit.

5. Select zone 1, select AIR FRY, set temperature to 155°C, and set time to 19 minutes. Select MATCH. Press the START/STOP button to begin cooking. (use a fork to gently pull back on a section in the thickest part of the filet. The salmon should flake away easily)
Cut and serve with an extra squeeze of lemon.

Fish Fingers and Mushy Peas

Serves : 4   Prep Time : 10 Mins   Cook Time : 20 mins

Ingredients

- 450g cod, haddock or any white fillets, thawed
- 5 tbsp plain flour
- 1 tbsp smoked paprika
- Zest of 1 small lemon
- 70g breadcrumbs
- 2 large eggs
- 500 g frozen garden peas
- Zest of 1 small lemon
- 100ml water
- Salt and pepper to taste

Method

1. In a shallow bowl add flour and season with salt and pepper, in another bowl add the egg, whisk, and add breadcrumbs in a third shallow bowl.

2. Slice the fish fillets lengthways into 2-cm wide fingers. Coat fish fingers with flour, then in the beaten egg, and finally in breadcrumbs, pressing to coat.

3. Insert a crisper plate into Zone 1 drawer. Place fish fingers in Zone 1 drawer, brush with oil, then insert drawer in unit.

4. With no crisping plate installed, add peas, water, lemon zest, salt, and pepper to Zone 2 drawer. Stir to combine. Insert drawer into the unit.

5. Select zone 1, select AIR FRY, set temperature to 190°C, and set time to 8 minutes. Select zone 1, select BAKE, set temperature to 200°C, and set time to 8 minutes. Select SYNC. Press the START/STOP button to begin cooking.

6. When Zone 1 and 2 time reaches 4 minutes, remove drawers from unit, flip the fish fingers using silicone-tipped tongs and stir the peas. Reinsert drawers to continue cooking.

7. When cooking is complete, remove drawers from unit and mash the peas with a fork. Serve fish fingers with mashed peas.

69

Fish Fingers and Mushy Peas

A classic family favourite, Simple to make, fuss-free and delicious.

Fish Cakes

Serves : 4   Prep Time : 10 Mins   Cook Time : 9 mins

Ingredients

- 340g cod or white fish fillets
- 70g breadcrumbs
- 2 tbsp finely chopped fresh coriander
- 2 tbsp mayonnaise
- 1 egg
- Salt and pepper to taste

Method

1. In a food processor add all ingredients and pulse a few times until crumbly. Shape mixture into 4 fish cakes.

2. Insert a crisper plate into both drawers. Brush plates with oil. Place fish cakes in Zone 1 and 2 drawers, brush with oil, then insert drawers in unit.

3. Select zone 1, select AIR FRY, set temperature to 190°C, and set time to 9 minutes. Select MATCH. Press the START/STOP button to begin cooking.

4. When Zone 1 reaches 5 minutes, remove drawers from unit and flip the fish cakes using silicone-tipped tongs. Reinsert drawers to continue cooking.

5. When cooking is complete, remove drawers from unit and serve fish cakes with lemon wedges.

Tuna Pasta Bake

Serves : 4   Prep Time : 5 Mins   Cook Time : 40 mins

Ingredients

- 200g dry fusilli pasta
- 1 tbsp butter
- 1 tbsp oil
- 1 onion, finely chopped
- 2 garlic cloves, minced
- 1 (400g) tin chopped tomatoes
- 250ml water
- 200g tinned tuna in oil, drained
- 75g grated mature cheddar cheese
- Salt and pepper to taste

Method

1. With no crisping plate installed, add butter, oil, garlic, tuna, pasta, tomatoes, salt, pepper and cheese to Zone 1 and 2 drawers (divide the amount between the two drawers). Stir to combine. Cover with tin foil. Insert drawers into the unit.

2. Select zone 1, select BAKE, set temperature to 180°C, and set time to 40 minutes. Select MATCH. Press the START/STOP button to begin cooking.

3. When cooking is complete, remove from unit, stir and serve

Garlic Butter Prawns

🛎 Serves : 4   🍜 Prep Time : 5 Mins   🍲 Cook Time : 10 mins

Ingredients

- 600g prawns, peeled and deveined
- 60ml melted butter
- 3 garlic cloves, minced
- Juice of 1 medium lemon
- Salt and pepper to taste

Method

1. With no crisping plate installed, add butter, garlic, prawns, lemon juice, , salt, and pepper to Zone 1 drawer. Stir to combine. Insert drawer into the unit.

2. Select zone 1, select BAKE, set temperature to 175°C, and set time to 10 minutes. Press the START/STOP button to begin cooking.

3. When time reaches 5 minutes in zone 1 drawer. Remove drawer and stir. Reinsert drawer in unit to continue cooking.
When cooking is complete, serve prawns with garlic butter sauce.

73

Prawns and Broccoli with Herbed Rice

Serves : 8   Prep Time : 10 Mins   Cook Time : 30 mins

Ingredients

Prawns and broccoli:

- 500g prawns, peeled and deveined
- 200g frozen broccoli florets, thawed
- 2 tbsp cornflour
- 2 tsp soy sauce
- 5 tbsp chicken stock
- 4 garlic cloves, minced
- 1 tsp white vinegar
- 1 tsp grated fresh ginger
- Salt and pepper to taste

Herbed rice:

- 500ml water
- 220g uncooked long grain rice
- 2 tbsp butter
- 1/2 tbsp parsley leaves, finely chopped
- 1/4 tbsp dried thyme
- Salt and pepper to taste

Method

1. With no crisping plate installed, add butter, garlic, prawns, lemon juice, , salt, and pepper to Zone 1 drawer. Stir to combine. Insert drawer into the unit.

2. With no crisping plate installed, add all rice ingredients. Stir. Insert drawer into the unit.

3. Select Zone 1, select AIR FRY, set temperature to 180°C, and set time to 15 minutes. Select Zone 2, select BAKE, set temperature to 200°C and set time for 30 minutes. Select SYNC. Press the START/PAUSE button to begin cooking.
When cooking is complete, remove drawers from unit. Fluff the rice with a fork and serve with prawns and broccoli.

Fish and Chips

Serves : 4   Prep Time : 10 Mins   Cook Time : 15 mins

Ingredients

Chips:

- 500g potatoes, peeled, cut into 1cm-thick chips and soaked in water for 30 minutes
- 2 tbsp oil
- Salt and pepper to taste

Fish:

- 500g cod fillets
- 60g plain flour
- 1 large egg, beaten
- 200g breadcrumbs

Method

1. In a shallow bowl add flour and season with salt and pepper, in another bowl add the beaten egg, and add breadcrumbs in a third shallow bowl. Coat fish with flour, then in egg, and finally in breadcrumbs, pressing to coat.

2. Rinse and pat potatoes dry. Coat the potatoes with oil and season with salt and pepper.

3. Insert a crisper plate into both drawers. Place the chips in Zone 1 drawer. Place the fish in Zone 2 drawer. Insert drawers into the unit.

4. Select Zone 1, select AIR FRY, set temperature to 200°C, and set time to 15 minutes. Select Zone 2, select BAKE, set temperature to 190°C and set time for 12 minutes. Select SYNC. Press the START/PAUSE button to begin cooking.

5. When time reaches 7 minutes in Zone 1 and 2 drawers, remove drawers from unit. Rearrange chips, and flip the fish. Reinsert drawers to continue cooking.
When cooking is complete, serve fish with chips.

75

Afternoon Tea

You're going to love these British afternoon tea ideas!

Hot Cross Buns

Serves : 8   Prep Time : 2 Hours   Cook Time : 25 mins

Ingredients

- 450g plain flour, divided
- 100g caster sugar, divided
- 70g unsalted butter
- Pinch of salt
- 180ml milk, warm
- 2 large egg, beaten
- 1/2 tsp ground cinnamon
- 1/2 tsp ground nutmeg
- 150g sultanas
- 2 1/4 tsp dried yeast

For the cross
- 70g plain flour mixed with 140ml water

For brushing
- Golden syrup

Method

1. In a bowl, add milk, yeast, and 2 tsp of caster sugar. Cover and sit for about 6 minutes.

2. After the 6 minutes, add remaining sugar, butter, eggs, salt, cinnamon, nutmeg, allspice, and 125g of the flour to the milk mixture. Mix with wooden spoon for 30 seconds.

3. Add the remaining flour and sultanas. Continue to knead for 3 more minutes. Dough will be a little sticky and soft. (If the dough is too sticky add more flour 1 tbsp at a time).

4. Leave the dough in the bowl and cover it for 1 hour to prove.

5. Punch the dough down to release the air. Divide dough into 8 pieces. Roll them into 8 balls.

6. Insert a crisper plate into both drawers. Place the buns in Zone 1 and 2 drawers. Cover with cling film and leave to prove for 30 minutes

7. Select zone 1, select BAKE, set temperature to 185°C, and set time to 25 minutes. Select MATCH. Press the START/STOP button to begin cooking.

8. When cooking is complete, remove from unit and allow to cool for a few minutes, then brush with golden syrup. Serve.

77

Cheese Scones

🍽 **Serves : 5**　　🍳 **Prep Time : 10 Mins**　　🍲 **Cook Time : 8 mins**

Ingredients

- 200g self-raising flour
- ¼ tsp mustard powder
- ½ tsp baking powder
- 100g frozen unsalted butter, grated
- 120g mature cheddar
- Pinch of salt
- Milk, as needed

Method

1. In a large bowl, add flour, salt, baking powder, mustard powder. Mix until combined. Add the butter, grated cheese and stir with spoon. Add milk gradually while kneading until a dough comes together (Do Not over knead).

2. Transfer the dough to a lightly floured surface, knead for 30 second and lightly roll into 3-cm in thickness. Cut out 5-cm scones until all dough is used up. Brush scones with milk.

3. Insert a crisper plate into both drawers. Place the scones in Zone 1 and 2 drawers, then insert drawers in unit.

4. Select zone 1, select BAKE, set temperature to 190°C, and set time to 8 minutes. Select MATCH. Press the START/STOP button to begin cooking.

5. When cooking is complete, remove from unit and serve warm .

Madeira Cake

Serves : 12   Prep Time : 10 Mins   Cook Time : 30 mins

Ingredients

- 190g unsalted butter, softened
- 190g sugar, divided
- Zest of 1 lemon
- 3 large eggs, room temperature
- 3 tbsp milk
- 270g plain flour
- 2 tsp baking powder

Method

1. In a bowl, add butter and sugar. Beat until creamy, add lemon zest and eggs one at a time while beating. Add the flour and baking powder to the butter mixture gradually while beating until combined.

2. Grease and line the Zone 1 drawer or 20x11-cm/ 1lb loaf cake tin with a piece of baking parchment. Pour the cake batter into the Zone 1 drawer. Insert drawer in unit.

3. Select zone 1, select BAKE, set temperature to 150°C and set time to 30 minutes. Press the START/STOP button to begin cooking.

4. When cooking is complete, cool in drawer 10 minutes before removing to a wire rack to cool completely. Slice and serve.

Bakewell Tart

Serves : 12   Prep Time : 1 Hour   Cook Time : 35 mins

Ingredients

For the pastry crust:

- 250g plain flour
- Pinch of salt
- 40g icing sugar
- 170g butter, frozen and grated
- 1 large egg yolk
- Ice cold water

For the filling:

- 250G unsalted butter, soft
- 200g caster sugar
- 1 ½ tsp almond extract
- 2 large eggs
- 250g almond flour
- Pinch of salt
- 30g plain flour
- 120g raspberry conserve
- 50g almond slices

Method

1. In a large bowl, add flour, salt, icing sugar. Mix until combined. Add the butter, and mix until it forms a coarse breadcrumbs. Add egg yolk, mix and water gradually and mix just until the dough comes together.

2. Divide the dough into 2 equal portions. Wrap in cling film and refrigerate for 30 minutes.

3. On a lightly floured surface, roll each dough large enough to line the base and sides of a 14-cm tart tins.

4. Gently press the dough into the sides of the tart tin. Prick the bottom with a fork and freeze for 30 minutes.

5. Line the pies with tin foil and fill with the two tarts with baking beans. Insert a crisper plate into both drawers. Place the tarts in Zone 1 and 2 drawers, then insert drawers in unit.

6. Select zone 1, select BAKE, set temperature to 180°C, and set time to 15 minutes. Select MATCH. Press the START/STOP button to begin cooking.

7. When time reaches 10 minutes in Zone 1 and 2 drawers, remove drawers from unit, remove the foil and baking beans and move the cookie sheet with tart shell to the upper rack. Reinsert drawers to continue cooking.

8. In a large bowl, add all filling ingredients (except almond slices) and beat with a hand mixer until combined and smooth.

9. When cooking is complete, remove the tarts from the drawers and spread each tart base with raspberry conserve and divide the filling mixture evenly between the two tarts , smooth the surface. Sprinkle with almond slices.

10. Place the tarts in Zone 1 and 2 drawers, then insert drawers in unit. Select zone 1, select BAKE, set temperature to 165℃, and set time to 20 minutes. Select MATCH. Press the START/STOP button to begin cooking.

When cooking is complete, remove from unit and cool completely before serving.

Apple Crumble Cake

Serves : 8   Prep Time : 10 Mins   Cook Time : 18 mins

Ingredients

For the Topping:

- 60g unsalted butter, melted
- 90g plain flour
- 60g caster sugar
- ¼ tsp ground cinnamon

For the Apple Cake:

- 240g plain flour
- 2 tsp baking powder
- 1 tsp ground cinnamon
- 115g unsalted butter, softened
- 150g caster sugar
- 3 medium eggs, room temperature
- 1 ½ tsp vanilla essence
- 80ml milk
- 3 Granny Smith apples peeled, thinly sliced and lightly coated with flour
- Pinch of salt
- Pinch of nutmeg

Method

1. In a bowl, add topping ingredients and mix until combined and crumbly.

2. In a bowl, add butter and sugar. Beat until creamy, add vanilla and eggs one at a time while beating. Add the flour and baking powder to the butter mixture gradually while beating until combined. Fold in the apples.

3. Grease 8 individual silicone muffin cups. Pour the cake batter into the muffin cups. Place muffin cups into Zone 1 and 2 drawers. Insert drawer in unit.

4. Select zone 1, select BAKE, set temperature to 160°C and set time to 18 minutes. Press the START/STOP button to begin cooking.

5. When cooking is complete, check the cakes are ready by inserting a skewer into the centre. If it comes out clean, remove the cakes from drawers and cool completely on a wire rack. If not, bake for another 3 minutes. Serve.

Apple Crumble Cake

This apple crumble cake is a buttery cinnamon flavoured cake that is loaded with fresh chopped apples and topped with crumble topping!

Mini Victoria Sponge Cakes

Serves : 6   Prep Time : 15 Mins   Cook Time : 15 mins

Ingredients

Cake :

- 120g butter, softened
- 120g caster sugar
- 2 medium eggs
- 120g self-raising flour
- 1 tsp baking powder
- 1 tbsp milk
- 1 tsp vanilla essence

Filling:

- 300ml double cream, whipped
- 4 tbsp raspberry/blueberry conserve

Method

1. In a bowl, add butter and sugar. Beat until creamy, add vanilla and eggs one at a time while beating. Add the flour and baking powder to the butter mixture gradually while beating until combined.

2. Grease individual six 7-cm cake tins, transfer the cake batter into the greased tins.

3. Insert a crisper plate into both drawers. Place the cake tins in Zone 1 and 2 drawers, then insert drawers in unit.

4. Select zone 1, select BAKE, set temperature to 160°C, and set time to 15 minutes. Select MATCH. Press the START/STOP button to begin cooking.

5. When cooking is complete, check the cakes are ready by inserting a skewer into the centre. If it comes out clean, remove the cakes from drawers and cool completely on a wire rack. If not, bake for another 3 minutes before testing again with a skewer.
When ready to serve, slice each cake in half fill with double cream and raspberry/blueberry conserve.

84

Mini Victoria Sponge Cakes

Everything is better in tiny form, and these tiny Victoria Sponge Cakes are no exception. These small cakes are fluffy, light, and the ideal bite size for Afternoon Tea

Welsh Cakes

Serves : 4   Prep Time : 15 Mins   Cook Time : 8 mins

Ingredients

- 110g self-raising flour
- 55g cold butter, cubed
- 30g caster sugar
- 1 handful of sultanas
- 1 large egg
- A few drops of milk, if needed

Method

1. In a bowl, add flour, salt and butter. Rub mixture using hands until resembles breadcrumbs. Stir in the sugar and the sultanas. Add the egg. Mix to a firm dough (if it is too dry, add some drops of milk gradually).

2. Transfer to a floured surface, roll out to 1 1/2-cm thickness, then cut into circles.

3. Insert a crisper plate into both drawers. Place the welsh cakes in Zone 1 and 2 drawers, brush with some melted butter, then insert drawers in unit.

4. Select zone 1, select BAKE, set temperature to 170°C, and set time to 8 minutes. Select MATCH. Press the START/STOP button to begin cooking.

5. When time reaches 5 minutes, remove drawers from unit. Flip the welsh cakes and reinsert drawers to continue cooking.
When cooking is complete, remove from unit and serve warm.

Custard Creams

Serves : 24 Custard Creams   Prep Time : 15 Mins   Cook Time : 12 mins

Ingredients

- 220g plain flour
- 220g unsalted butter, softened
- 80g icing sugar
- 100g No added sugar custard powder

For the filling:

- 100g butter, softened
- 250g icing sugar
- 1 lemon zest
- 1 tbsp lemon juice

Method

1. In a bowl, add the butter and beat until creamy, then beat in the icing sugar, then mix in the other ingredients until combined and form a dough.

2. Transfer dough to a work surface and roll it into a log and cut into 48 equal portions. Roll each portion into a ball and flatten with a fork slightly.

3. Insert a crisper plate into both drawers. Place the Custard Creams 3-cm apart in Zone 1 and 2 drawers, brush with some melted butter, then insert drawers in unit.

4. Select zone 1, select BAKE, set temperature to 170°C, and set time to 8 minutes. Select MATCH. Press the START/STOP button to begin cooking. When cooing is complete, remove from unit and set aside for 30 minutes to cool.

5. In a bowl, add the filling ingredients and beat until light and creamy. Spread the icing on each biscuit half (24 half) and sandwich together with remaining biscuits.

Bara Brith

Makes 10 large slices Prep Time : 15 Mins Cook Time : 25 mins

Ingredients

- 400g mixed dried fruit, soaked overnight in 300ml hot black tea and 100g brown sugar
- 250g self-raising flour
- 1 tsp mixed spice
- 1 egg, beaten

Method

1. Add flour, mixed spices and egg into the bowl of soaked mixed fruit. Mix until combined.

2. Grease and two 450g/1lb loaf tins with baking paper. Pour the mixture evenly into loaf tins.

3. With no crisping plates installed. Place loaf tins into Zone 1 and 2 drawers. Insert drawers in unit.

4. Select zone 1, select BAKE, set temperature to 165°C, and set time to 25 minutes. Select MATCH. Press the START/STOP button to begin cooking (use a skewer to check the bread. If it comes out clean, the bread is ready. If not, bake for a further 5 minutes covering with tin foil).

5. When cooking is complete, remove from unit and store for 2 days before eating.

Sticky Toffee Pudding

🔔 **Makes 6 puddings**   🥣 **Prep Time : 10 Mins**   🍲 **Cook Time : 25 mins**

Ingredients

- 4 tbsp golden syrup
- 70g soft butter
- 60g brown sugar
- 2 medium eggs
- 190g self-raising flour
- 1/2 tsp baking powder
- 200g dried dates, pitted, chopped and soaked in 200ml boiling water for 30 minutes
- 2 tbsp milk

Method

1. Grease six 180ml/4oz ramekins. Mash the soaked dates.

2. In a bowl, add butter and sugar, mix using a hand mixer until creamy. Add flour, baking powder, eggs and cinnamon. mix with spoon until combined. Add mashed dates mixture and milk. mix with spoon until combined. Fill the ramekins 2/3 way up with the pudding.

3. With crisping plates installed. Place pudding into Zone 1 and 2 drawers. Insert drawers in unit.

4. Select zone 1, select BAKE, set temperature to 160°C, and set time to 20 minutes. Select MATCH. Press the START/STOP button to begin cooking (use a skewer to check the pudding. If it comes out clean, the pudding is ready. If not, bake for a further 5 minutes covered with foil).

5. When cooing is complete, remove from unit and turn upside down on serving plate. Serve warm.

6. For the butterscotch sauce:
On a pan over medium heat, add 50g butter,150g brown sugar, 300ml double cream. Stir and bring to a boil. Simmer for 2 minutes, then remove from heat. Serve warm with the sticky toffee pudding.

Hobnob Biscuits

Makes : 20 biscuits   Prep Time : 15 Mins   Cook Time : 25 mins

Ingredients

- 150g self-raising flour
- 100g caster sugar
- 150g unsalted butter
- 1 tbsp milk
- 2 tbsp golden syrup
- 1/2 tsp bicarbonate of soda
- 120g jumbo oats

Method

1. In a large bowl, add sugar and butter. Beat with a mixer until light and creamy. Add the milk, golden syrup, and beat.

2. Add the flour and bicarbonate of soda into the butter mixture and mix using a spoon. Add the oats and mix. Refrigerate for 10 minutes.

3. Divide the dough into 25g spoonfuls. Quickly roll into balls.

4. With crisping plates installed. Place biscuits into Zone 1 and 2 drawers. Insert drawers in unit.

5. Select zone 1, select BAKE, set temperature to 140°C, and set time to 25 minutes. Select MATCH. Press the START/STOP button to begin cooking .

6. When cooing is complete, remove from unit and let set for 10 min. Transfer Biscuits to a cooling rack until completely cool.

Carrot Cake Loaf

Serves: 6   Prep Time : 10 Mins   Cook Time : 20 mins

Ingredients

Carrot Cake:

- 150 light brown sugar
- 150ml vegetable oil
- 100g grated carrots
- 100 walnuts, finely chopped
- 2 large eggs
- 150g plain flour
- 1 tsp bicarbonate of soda
- 1 tsp baking powder
- ½ tsp cinnamon
- 1/4 tsp ground nutmeg
- Pinch of salt

Icing:

- 115g cream cheese, room temperature
- 2 tbsp unsalted butter
- 200g icing sugar

Method

1. In a large bowl, add flour, baking powder, bicarbonate of soda, cinnamon, nutmeg, salt. Mix and set aside.

2. In another bowl, add eggs, sugar and oil. Beat with a hand mixer until combined.

3. Pour the egg mixture into the flour mixture. Mix until combined. Add the grated carrots, walnuts and mix with a wooden spoon or spatula until combined.

4. Grease two 450g/1-lb loaf tins and pour the cake mixture into the greased tins.

5. With no crisping plates installed. Place loaf tins into Zone 1 and 2 drawers. Insert drawer in unit.

6. Select zone 1, select BAKE, set temperature to 165°C, and set time to 20 minutes. Select MATCH. Press the START/STOP button to begin cooking (use a skewer to check the cake. If it comes out clean, the cake is ready. If not, bake for a further 5 minutes covering with tin foil).

7. When cooing is complete, remove from unit and let cool completely.

8. In a bowl, add all icing ingredients and beat with hand mixer (or with a whisk) until smooth. Do Not over mix the icing. Spread the icing on top of the cake sprinkle with walnuts & carrots. Slice, serve.

91

Yorkshire Parkin

Serves: 16 **Prep Time : 15 Mins** **Cook Time : 1 Hour**

Ingredients

- 120g porridge oats
- 90g plain flour
- 1 1/2 tsp baking powder
- 2 tsp ground ginger
- 1 tsp allspice
- Pinch of salt
- 180ml black treacle
- 60ml golden syrup
- 30g brown sugar
- 120g butter
- 1 large egg , lightly beaten
- 2 tbsp whole milk

Method

1. Grease two 450/1-lb loaf tins. In bowl, add flour,oats, allspice, ground ginger, salt and baking powder. Mix.

2. In a pan over medium heat, add sugar, black treacle, golden syrup, butter. Heat until melted and remove from the heat. Let it cool for 5 minutes.

3. Pour butter/treacle mixture into flour and mix until combined. Add the egg and milk and stir until combined and smooth. Pour the batter evenly into the loaf tins.

4. With no crisping plates installed, place loaf tins into Zone 1 and 2 drawers.

5. Select zone 1, select BAKE, set temperature to 140°C, and set time to 50 minutes. Select MATCH. Press the START/STOP button to begin cooking (use a skewer to check the cake. If it comes out clean, the cake is ready. If not, bake for a further 10 minutes covering with tin foil).

6. Let the cake cool then invert onto a plate. Cut into squares and serve.

Irish Soda Bread

🔔 **Serves: 20**   🍲 **Prep Time : 20 Mins**   🍳 **Cook Time : 10 mins**

Ingredients

- 480g plain flour
- 120g butter, softened
- 4 tbsp caster sugar
- 1 tsp bicarbonate of soda
- 1 tbsp baking powder
- 240ml buttermilk
- Pinch of salt
- 1 egg

For brushing:

- 60g butter, melted
- 40ml buttermilk

Method

1. In a small bowl, add the melted butter, 40ml buttermilk, mix and set aside.

2. In a large bowl, add flour, butter, sugar, salt, bicarbonate of soda, baking powder. Mix until combined. Add the buttermilk, egg and knead until a dough is formed. Divide the dough into 2 equal balls.

3. Insert the crisper plates in Zone 1 and 2 drawers. Brush with oil. Place one loaf on each crisper plate. Using a sharp knife, slash the tops (X). Brush with butter/buttermilk mixture. Insert drawers in unit.

4. Select Zone 1, select BAKE, set temperature to 180°C and set time to 20 minutes. Select MATCH. Press START/STOP to begin.

5. When time reaches 10 minutes, remove drawers and brush each loaf with butter/buttermilk mixture. Reinsert drawers in unit to continue cooking.
When cooking is complete, remove from unit and let cool, then slice and serve.

93

INDEX

AFTERNOON TEA

Printed in Great Britain
by Amazon